MONSTERS
CAUGHT ON FILM

AMAZING EVIDENCE OF LAKE MONSTERS,
BIGFOOT & OTHER STRANGE BEASTS

DR MELVYN WILLIN

D&C
David and Charles

David & Charles is an F+W Media Inc. company
4700 East Galbraith Road
Cincinnati, OH 45236

First published in the UK in 2010
First published in the US in 2010

ISBN-13: 978-0-7153-3774-5 hardback
ISBN-10: 0-7153-3774-2 hardback

Printed in China by RR Donnelley
for David & Charles
Brunel House, Newton Abbot, Devon

Commissioning Editor: Neil Baber
Editor: Verity Muir
Senior Designer: Jodie Lystor
Project Editor: Emily Pitcher
Production Controller: Kelly Smith

David & Charles publish high quality books on a wide range of
subjects. For more great book ideas visit: www.rubooks.co.uk

Contents

INTRODUCTION

Monsters caught on film? Perhaps this title needs some explanation before exploring the following material. In this book I wished to broaden the remit to include both merely apparent or illusory creatures but also the possibility of non-hallucinatory phenomena, the origin of which may be natural or beyond our current scientific understanding. Photographic examples will include possibly fraudulently produced manifestations via trick photography or the use of stage props and, most importantly of all, images that seem to defy normal explanations – perhaps organisms that are either alive or have at some stage lived, but seem to defy biological classification. Examples of these will be sought from the animal kingdom and will include various hairy hominids, furry predators, flying anomalies and aquatic beasts. Other examples may even have an extra-terrestrial source. The ape-like creatures will be represented by old favourites such as the Abominable Snowmen, Sasquatch and Yeti. The substantial photographic evidence of four-footed-furry-felines demands the inclusion of a host of cats as well as some dogs. Flying abnormalities are difficult to capture but there are a few intriguing images to discuss, including a controversial pterodactyl.

On the other side, water-based beasts are well represented with many fascinating pictures of plesiosaur-like dinosaurs from Loch Ness and elsewhere, as well as undisputed living prehistoric examples such as the coelacanth. The extra-terrestrial inclusions are the most difficult to come to terms with, but in a universe of almost unmeasurable vastness I believe it is unwise to be too dogmatic about our exclusive position in terms of life forms.

The problem with such a cryptozoological-type exploration is where to draw the line. This has been dictated in many examples by the lack of photographic evidence. Tempting though it was to use mythological creatures, especially when they are such a part of the human imagination (unicorns, gorgons, dragons, minotaurs) I had to find mainly photos and not use illustrations to stay true to the nature of the book. Similarly the images of dinosaurs were kept to a minimum since they would appear to be particularly elusive when it comes to a photo shoot! As always one's own belief system has to come into play in such circumstances and I would urge the readers of this book (and the others in the series) to try to keep an open mind – but not so open that one's brains fall out!

Experiences are subjective and always open to change as more knowledge is accepted or rejected. Your 'boggle' threshold may well be different to mine, so let us explore these images in a spirit of learning and enjoyment, lest future generations are appalled at our naïveté or intransigence.

MONSTERS OF THE DEEP

Mankind has explored outside of our world with some success – reaching the moon and sending
equipment even further afield to distant planets in the galaxy, but what about our own precious
environment? The seas still hide many mysteries in their greatest depths where humans could not survive
without the most specialist equipment, and even then only for short periods of time. The seas are so vast
that they could never be properly examined anyway – the Pacific Ocean alone covers forty per cent of the
world's total sea area. Its greatest breadth is 10,000 miles (16,000km) and 6,800 miles (11,000km) long. The
average depth is approximately 4,000m (13,000ft), but drops to a staggering 11,000 m (36,000ft) in some
areas (the Marianas Trench). In these circumstances is it not somewhat likely that there will be things
hidden there that we do not know about despite our advances in technology and knowledge?

In this chapter we shall explore different watery worlds, and many questions will remain unanswered. For
instance, what was the evil-smelling, rotting carcass that was hauled onto the *Zuiyo Maru* trawler in 1977
off the coast of New Zealand? The crew certainly believed they had discovered something unidentified. The
'sea serpent', caught off the coast of England in 1897 was almost certainly a hoax, but if there were not
genuine examples of unknown living things swimming our seas why would people be willing to accept
the possibility of such organisms existing? With the exotically named Kraken we are very much into the
world of the monster, but one must add that this particular beast really does exist and has been captured
and studied at length. The sceptics would have poured scorn on the idea of giant sea monsters lurking in
the depths of our oceans two hundred years ago, but the sailors were right and the sceptics have been

quietened. This is similarly true concerning the enormous oarfish and the beaked whale, both of which are alive and well and available for scientific scrutiny. The latter has been mistaken for a surviving plesiosaur, which links comfortably with the Loch Ness Monster. You can view several photos of what has been seen in Loch Ness and make your own mind up about the veracity of the photos and the reports that have accompanied them. Whatever your conclusions the place is certainly atmospheric and the loch is big and deep enough to harbour something unknown or unusual. It may not be the prehistoric animal we would like it to be, but the possibility of a species of fish or mammal living there that is currently unknown to science is equally intriguing.

Of course, Nessie has its look-a-likes around Britain and the rest of the world. We can start in Cornwall with the frightening Morgawr, before setting off to Lake Champlain on the USA/Canadian border to hope for a sighting of Champ the resident monster, or Lake Okanagan, British Columbia for a meeting with Ogopogo – all members perhaps of Nessie's extended family. It has been suggested that these sightings can all be put down to either floating vegetation or logs, seals or otters, hoaxes or exaggeration. Many people believe that giant sturgeons may have been wrongly identified as such creatures. So look carefully and see if you can see any similarities between these massive fish and the photos of our various monsters. From monstrous, unidentifiable, decaying carcasses to the parasitic sea lampreys, gorge yourself on some of the findings that have baffled and marvelled scientists for centuries, and make your own decision about what they really are...

The Zuiyo Maru Sea Monster

On April 25th, 1977 the Japanese fishing boat *Zuiyo Maru* was trawling for mackerel in the Pacific Ocean east of Christchurch, New Zealand when crew members landed the rotten, stinking carcass of an unidentified creature. The ship's captain was concerned that the haul might contaminate the rest of his catch and so ordered for it to be measured and photographed, before being slung back into the sea. The body was measured by a crew member at 6m (20ft), with the head being 45cm (18in) long, and each of the four fins measuring 1m (3ft).

'Crew members landed the rotten, stinking carcass of an unidentified creature'

The trawler's crew believed the carcass to be that of a plesiosaur – a Mesozoic four-flippered, carnivorous reptile that lurked beneath the surface of the water hunting for prey. Scientists, however, identified it as a basking shark or whale. Differences of opinion naturally followed, with two Japanese professors (Yoshinori Imaizumi and Toshio Kasuya) disagreeing with the classification and declaring it proof that plesiosaurs still exist. With the physical evidence disposed of another haul of this kind would be necessary to prove that these creatures still patrol our oceans, rather than this being an example of a dramatic new marine discovery.

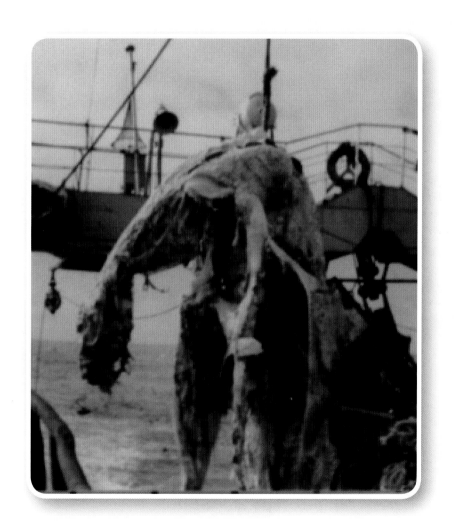

A Sea Serpent or a Fishy Tale?

Details about this photograph are sparse, but the information to hand informs us that this 'sea serpent' was caught off the English coast in 1897. There have been claims of sea serpent sightings for hundreds of years, and cryptozoologists claim that the sheer number of claimed sightings and similarities in accounts of their appearance are proof of these creatures' existence. No credible physical evidence has ever been recorded however, and the sightings have been put down to misidentification of oarfish or whales. Is this image a ruse, or have these men genuinely captured a rare specimen that defies current scientific knowledge? The disembodied arm in the centre of the image is the result of a section of the photograph being folded.

The date of the photo rules out digital manipulation of the image, but it has been suggested that the placement of the men's hands conceals possible joints in a model. The lack of information about this photograph should also make one cautious about drawing any conclusions. Wouldn't it be wonderful if we were wrong, though, and this wasn't an innocent jape?

'Is this image a ruse, or have these men genuinely captured a rare specimen?'

The Kraken

In the late 18th century Bishop Pontoppidan of Bergen, Norway wrote of a report made under oath by Captain Lorenz von Ferry and other witnesses, describing the appearance of a giant creature with 'seven or eight coils [that] could be seen above the water' off the coast in Norway. The giant squid, or kraken (meaning something rotten and twisted in Scandinavian) is the stuff of folklore, and is arguably one of the most infamous creatures of the deep. But does it really exist?

The stuff of fiction, the kraken has appeared in many films, including *The Clash of the Titans*, *Pirates of the Caribbean 2* and in Jules Verne's book *20,000 Leagues Under the Sea*. In 1857 this enigmatic cephalopod was classified by the Danish zoologist Johan Japetus Steenstrup as *Architeuthis*, but its existence was still hotly disputed. The discovery of some remains along the rocky coast of Newfoundland in the late 19th century finally silenced the sceptics. The findings indicated tentacles of over 9m (30ft) and a body some 18m (60ft) long and 3m (10ft) wide. Disputes still abound surrounding the size these creatures can grow to, with some suggesting a length of 27.5m (90ft) in order to challenge their arch enemy, the sperm whale. Tales of monsters at sea are nothing new – but this reputedly stinking creature bucks the trend by actually existing.

'A giant creature with seven or eight coils that could be seen above the water'

THE GIANT SQUID

The Oarfish

On March 3rd, 1860 a 'sea serpent' was washed up on a beach in Bermuda. Later identified as an oarfish, this enormous fish was held responsible for numerous mariners' claims of sea serpents and monster sightings. Measuring some 15m (50ft) in length and weighing in excess of 272kg (600lbs), these scale-less, gelatinous fish are the stuff of many a fisherman's tale.

Much more is now known about the species. The oarfish, *Regalecus glesne* can be found in the eastern Atlantic and Mediterranean oceans, although there are unsubstantiated claims that one was caught off the coast of North Yorkshire, UK, by an angler using squid as bait, in 2003. The fish tend to beach when ill or dying, thus enabling scientists to find out much more about them. They mainly live at depths of around 914m (3,000ft), and sightings or study of healthy, live oarfish are rare. These toothless fish are likely to feed on plankton, small crustaceans and squid, and have achieved *Guinness World Record* fame for being the longest bony fish in the world.

'These scale-less, gelatinous fish are the stuff of many a fisherman's tale'

Plesiosaur or Beaked Whale?

The head and partial body of this creature caused much excitement when they were washed up on the rocks at Natural Bridges State Beach – later known as 'Moore's Beach' after Charles Moore who discovered the creature – at Monterey Bay, Santa Cruz, California in 1925. The curious find was dubbed 'Moore's Beach Monster'. Similar remains were found on California's Ocean Beach in July 2003. Is this proof that plesiosaurs still exist, or is there a less controversial explanation?

The 1925 remains were collected and examined by scientists from the California Academy of Sciences, who identified the mystery creature as a rare beaked whale (*Berardius bairdii*). This identification did not stop speculation, however, with some people continuing to believe that it was a plesiosaur. These included E. L. Wallace, an ex-president of the Natural History Society of British Columbia, who further believed that it had been preserved in ice for millions of years before melting had set it free. This cetacean is one of many creatures that inhabit deep water and are rarely seen, spending much of their time diving for squid and deepwater fish far off the coast. How many more organisms from these habitats are waiting to be discovered, and what will we learn from them?

'The curious find was dubbed 'Moore's Beach Monster'

Nessie Galore

The Loch Ness Monster is probably one of the most famous cases of cryptozoology. The possibility of there being a monster living in a Scottish lake was first recorded as early as c.565AD. Modern day public attention was brought to the subject in 1933 when, in a letter to the *Inverness Courier* published on August 3rd, Mr and Mrs George Spicer described having seen a 'most extraordinary form of animal' cross the road in front of their car while they were driving round the loch. Two further sightings emerged that year, including one from a motorcyclist who claimed to have almost collided with the creature one moonlit night. The Spicers described the monster as being 'about 1m (4ft) high and 8m (25ft) long, with a narrow neck, slightly thicker than an elephant's trunk and as long as the 3–4m (10–12ft) width of the road. The idea that this monster could possibly be a plesiosaur was mooted in 1933, and the debate has raged ever since.

> 'A motorcyclist claimed to have almost collided with the creature one moonlit night'

Accounts of sightings are largely anecdotal, while scientific evidence centres around questionable sonar readings. Proven counterfeit photographs have done little to help the cause for Nessie's existence. Misidentification or pure fantasy are the other explanations given for witness accounts, with eels, cormorants, deer, vegetation, debris or trees held up as the true source. Every opinion and sighting can be countered with an opposing viewpoint, and folklore, myth and tradition could arguably be held responsible for the continued enthusiasm surrounding the subject. Perhaps one needs to visit the loch to decide for oneself, but wouldn't it be wonderful if it was true?

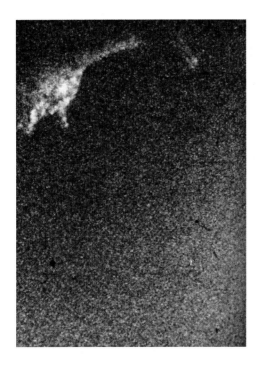

This image was taken by a team of researchers from the Academy of Applied Science, Boston in 1975 using a sonar-guided system. It allegedly shows the neck and body of an unidentified creature in the loch, with a neck some 2–3.5m (7–12ft) long. Sceptics argue that computer enhancement or vegetative debris could have been responsible.

This photo, taken in 1933, was said to show a creature about 12m (40ft) long with dark, shiny skin. Unfortunately it is often referred to as the 'Labrador' photo, since the head of a dog can be imagined facing the camera.

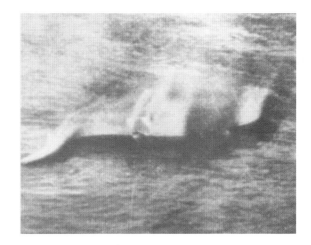

Probably the most famous of all the Nessie images is the so-called
'Surgeon' photograph, taken by R. K. Wilson on April 1, 1934. Despite the
significant date on which the photograph was taken (All Fools Day), any
hint of a hoax was largely ignored because the photo had been taken
by such a respectable surgeon. It has been claimed that the image was
created by photographing a toy submarine with an attachment. Further
evidence arose in 1994 that suggested a hoax.

Lachlan Stuart, a Forestry Commission worker, took this single image in July 1951. It appears to show three humps on the south shore of Loch Ness, although Lachlan maintains that there was also a head and neck that he did not manage to capture. Sceptics claim that these are rocks in relatively shallow water.

The 'McNab' photo of July 1955 shows an alleged sighting in the most popular part of the loch for Nessie sightings, close to the ruins of Urquhart Castle. Tim Dinsdale, one of the leading investigators, claimed that Peter MacNab, a bank manager, used a 'hand-held camera with six-inch telephoto lens attached' to capture the creature.

This photo, taken by the eccentric self-styled psychic Anthony 'Doc' Shiels in May 1977, has courted considerable controversy concerning its veracity. The clarity of the image is said to indicate a hoax, with the head probably super-imposed.

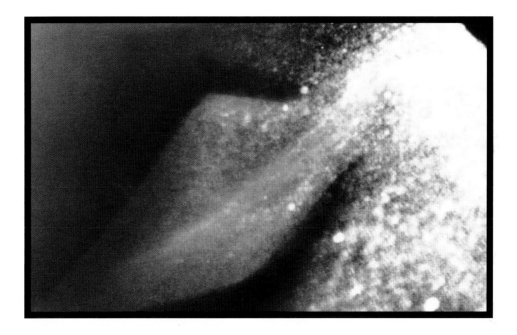

This underwater photo was taken in August 1972 by the
Academy of Applied Science and is generally known as
the 'flipper'. Arguments about its authenticity range from it
showing the genuine flipper of a plesiosaur-like creature to a
computer-enhanced image of vegetation.

Morgawr
– The Cornish Sea Giant

'Mary F' (as she wishes to be known) took these two photos in February 1976 at Rosemullion Head, near Falmouth off the coast of Cornwall in England. In her own words, as cited in Bord, 1981:

> *'It looked like an elephant waving its trunk, but the trunk was a long neck with a small head on the end, like a snake's head. It had lumps on the back which moved in a funny way. The colour was black or very dark brown, and the skin seemed like a sealion's…the animal frightened me. I would not like to see it any closer…'*

A number of other sightings have been documented, including accounts by local fishermen who would certainly have been aware of the difference between a large seal and an unknown sea creature. Other reports from holidaymakers were treated with less sympathy as the tourist season set in. Anthony 'Doc' Shiels (who claims to photograph aquatic monsters yet says he doesn't believe that they exist) allegedly had at least two sightings of Morgawr which he failed to clearly photograph. His companion David Clarke, the editor of *Cornish Life* magazine, also failed to capture the animal when his camera malfunctioned. This is curiously reminiscent of psychic activities which also seem to adversely affect recording technology, either suggesting human error or a genuine disturbance in some unknown energy field. What we are left with is a pair of intriguing photos of what might be an unknown creature that has somehow defied evolution in surviving to this day… or a case of over active imaginations.

'The trunk was a long neck with a small head on the end'

The Champ

This famous photo was taken in 1977 by Sandra Mansi on Lake Champlain which borders Vermont and New York State – the lake itself was named after the explorer Samuel de Champlain and is the largest body of water in the USA apart from the famous Great Lakes. She writes that her fiancé and two children all witnessed a disturbance in the lake, followed by the sighting of several minutes and her subsequent photo. She did not have other photos and did not keep the negative. There have subsequently been over 300 claimed sightings.

Inevitably the 'monster' has been linked with Nessie, inferring a plesiosaur origin, while other similarities include the commercial and tourist interest. There is an annual Champ Day celebration on August 3rd. In 2002 the *Skeptical Inquirer* magazine launched an investigative expedition which concluded that there is 'not a single piece of convincing evidence for Champ's existence, but there are many reasons against it'. The reporters cited sturgeon, which can reach lengths of 5.5m (18ft) and driftwood, among other possibilities, as the true identity. A hoax would have taken considerable preparation and seems unlikely in this instance, but the subsequent disposal of the negative makes it impossible to check for image tampering. Some answers to the mystery have included a sand bar with debris on it, an out of perspective large bird or animal or, as the many people who have sighted it would claim, a giant unknown water monster!

'A hoax would have taken considerable preparation and seems unlikely in this instance'

Lake Champlain is a 125-mile (201km)-
long body of fresh water and is the ideal
habitat for a large aquatic mammal. It is
122m (400ft) deep in places, and holds
a diverse population of fish and other
animals for sustenance. If only Sandra
Mansi could remember the exact part of
the lake she took this picture, we might be
able to believe that this really is a scientific
phenomenon and plesiosaurs do still exist.

The Champ

'It was as big as my thigh,' said fisherman Peter Bodette. 'I'm 100 per cent sure of what we saw. I'm not 100 per cent sure of what it was.' The fishermen were Champ sceptics before this sighting.

www.abcnews.com

American news channel ABC News obtained exclusive video footage of something just under the surface of the lake that some say may be Champ. The video was taken by two fishermen with a digital camera.

The Giant Acipenseridae

Looking at this photo one can see why the sturgeon might be responsible for sightings of so-called sea monsters. They usually live near the bottom of rivers, lakes and near coasts and rarely surface; they have elongated bodies, no scales and can reach 5.5m (18ft) in length. They have inhabited our waters for approximately two hundred million years with little change to their morphology, and they can live for up to one hundred years. They can be found around the world, and have been protected by royalty including Frederick the Great and Edward II of England. There are over twenty species belonging to this Acipenseridae family. The harvesting of their highly-prized roe, which is traditionally used for caviar, has resulted in them being designated an endangered species. If this species' existence was not confirmed by science, would you have any qualms if you were told about them lurking at the bottom of your nearest body of water?

Details about this photo shown here are scant, but it allegedly shows a sturgeon found dead in Lake Washington, Seattle, in November 1987. It was found floating on the surface of the lake, and was 3.4m (11ft) long and weighed over 420kg (900lb). the lack of teeth indicates that sturgeons would probably not attack a human, but they have been known to swallow whole salmon, so a child might just prove tempting.

'The lack of teeth indicates that sturgeons would probably not attack a human'

The 'Pogos' –
Manipogo and Ogopogo

There are a number of similarities between these two lake-dwelling creatures from Canada and North America. Manipogo, probably named after the more famous Ogopogo, is claimed to be an inhabitant of Lake Manitoba, north of Winnipeg, Canada. Ogopogo, or naitakas, is the so-called monster of Lake Okanagan, British Columbia, USA. There are a number of reports from Eskimos of these animals, which some suggest may be related to folklore beliefs of gods of the water. Claims of the monsters' existence have received considerable scrutiny since the earliest reports in 1860, while the photographic evidence of both creatures indicates a long, snake-like body.

The image (right) was taken on August 12th, 1962 at Ogopogo by two fishermen who claimed that the creature resembled 'a large black snake or eel' moving at considerable speed. They estimated the hump was about two feet long. The images (far right, top and bottom) are part of a set of pictures taken by Ed Fletcher of Vancouver on August 3rd, 1976.

'The fishermen claimed that the creature resembled "a large black snake or eel" moving at considerable speed'

Since then there have been numerous photos taken at both locations, and even video film which, as is often the case, was heavily disputed. There have been various inconclusive scientific expeditions to the lakes, and books and festivals have been devoted to the creatures. What the images show is still undecided – an extinct whale or reptile? A living sturgeon? Overlapping waves or vegetative debris? Or are they simply good, old fashioned hoaxes? You decide.

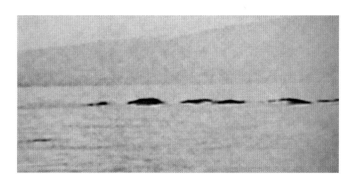

Sea Monster

In 2007 the decomposing remains of this unidentified creature were cast ashore in the Republic of Guinea, West Africa. It was described as having 'a hairy body, four paws and a tail'. The find has, to this day, baffled scientists who are unable to confirm its identity.

A number of suggestions have been made about what this find could be. These range from a decaying woolly mammoth, that had been preserved in ice that subsequently melted and released it, or a whale. The only identity that can really be given to it is that of a 'globster', a phrase coined by Ivan T. Sanderson in 1962. The word is used to describe any unidentifiable, organic decaying mass that is washed up on a shoreline. An unsatisfactory conclusion, perhaps, but who knows what mystery will come ashore from our great oceans next? So much is unknown, we can only hope that something else will come to light to help us identify what this creature really is.

'The decomposing remains had a hairy body, four paws and a tail'

Aquatic Vampires

The lamprey's method of attack is somewhat gruesome – it rips a hole in its fish prey, and then attaches itself to the victim to suck out its vital fluids using a long tongue. An anti-coagulant in the saliva of the lamprey ensures that the victim's blood keeps flowing until it finally dies from blood loss or infection. In folklore they have appeared as 'nine-eyed eels' from a counting of their seven external gill slits on each side, with one eye and the nostril.

The *Petromyzon marinus* is a long, vertebrate, scale-less fish that resembles an eel in appearance, with a circular teeth-filled mouth. It can be found in freshwater lakes, rivers and seas around the world. They have many different colours and grow up to 0.9m (3ft) in length. Its primitive cartilaginous skeleton is less easily fossilized than bone, but fossils have been found as far back as the Carboniferous or Devonian periods – some 360 million years ago. These parasites have a similar life cycle to salmon, being born in inland rivers, maturing in the ocean before returning to the rivers to spawn. Roman, Viking and Medieval Britons regarded river and sea lampreys as delicacies in their feasts, and they can still be found on menus in south west Europe, should you fancy sampling this delicious treat for yourself.

'It rips a hole in its prey and then attaches itself to the victim to suck out its vital fluids using a long tongue'

MYSTERIOUS PREDATORS

Forget fictitious predators and gruesome monsters of books and film. The animals here are real and much closer to home – have a look out of your window and you might just spot one now. These predators are likely to be hostile to humans at best and fully carnivorous at worst, so give them a wide berth.

We are pet lovers renowned for our affection towards animals and are therefore unlikely to mistake a domestic pet for an animal that ought to be in a zoo or roaming wild in Africa. Despite this there are many sightings each year of cats and dogs that cannot be accounted for in the usual ways. They are often much too big and behave in ways that are not in accordance with normal feline or canine behaviour. There are far too many reports for them to all be escaped animals from zoos, discarded exotic pets, hoaxes or wrong interpretations. Sometimes the sightings can be fleeting before the animal senses the presence of a human and escapes. From thousands of available photographs we present just a handful here to show you the very best – and most baffling – occurrences. In many cases the integrity of the witnesses and photographers cannot be easily questioned and digital manipulation would seem pointless. With the various authorities adamant that a mundane explanation can allay peoples' fears and the public's excitement and scrutiny, the truth behind the contents of these photos is often never discovered or proved.

For the second part of the chapter we return to the sea and meet up with a couple of dangerous and worryingly real creatures. The idea of being stung by a jellyfish is bad enough at any time, but the thought of killer Portugese man-of-war specimens surrounding some coastal areas where they should not be found is far more worrying, yet appears to be the case. It is said that a veritable armada of them has appeared in British waters over the past three consecutive years, with sixty reports received by the Marine Conservation Society. It seems that some rather dangerous sharks have also started visiting waters away from their usual hunting grounds. These fish are not figments of someone's imagination and neither are they floating logs or hoaxes…they are completely real, and although you are unlikely to be attacked by *Jaws* while paddling at the beach, nevertheless, one must heed the warnings given.

Perhaps these occurrences are a sign of things to come as our climates get warmer. Maybe it really is only a matter of time before Great Whites are troubling surfers closer to home as they do in Australia? What other beasts will stray into foreign lands where they don't usually go and, more importantly, what will happen to make us discover them? Who knows what's really lurking beneath the surface, or in the twilight wilderness,

The Whitley Dog

In June 2007 Martin Whitley was leading a group on a hawking expedition in Devon, England, when one of his clients spotted a strange animal nearby:

'I was flying a hawk on Dartmoor with some American clients, when one of them pointed out this creature. It was walking along a path about 200yds (600ft) away from us. It was black and grey and comparable in size to a miniature pony. It had very thick shoulders, a long, thick tail with a blunt end, and small round ears. Its movement appeared feline; then "bear-like" sprang to mind…'

Experts quickly discounted the creature being a big cat, so what could it possibly be? A large, feral dog? Or a mis-identified farm animal? There are many accounts of sightings of large black dogs in England, including a contemporaneous report from Bungay, Suffolk, dated 1577, and a very detailed account of an attack on a secluded farmhouse on the southern edge of Dartmoor in 1972. Whether or not Mr Whitley is correct about the identity of the creature, the photo is nevertheless intriguing. Perhaps its closeness to Hound Tor – made famous by Sir Arthur Conan Doyle's *Hound of the Baskervilles* – is a further clue in the quest to discover what lurks in Britain's more remote landscapes.

'It had very thick shoulders and small round ears'

Danny Camping, from the British Big Cats
Association, felt that the creature was unlikely
to be feline. He said: 'I wouldn't completely rule
out a dog or a pony, but my money would be on
a hairy wild boar.'

www.bbc.co.uk

The Whitley Dog

Is it porcine, a lost pet, a feral feline or a case of mistaken identity for a farm animal? You decide! All we know for certain is that the appearance of this creature has helped to boost the tourism trade in the area, and that Mr Whitley's 'beast tours' are proving to be very popular.

Surrey Puma

Reports of strange felines on the loose in Surrey, England, are not unusual and date back to the 18th century. The discovery of a severely lacerated bullock in 1962 led to another flurry of reported sightings, and a paw print that was found nearby was identified by experts at London Zoo as that of a puma – and a large one at that. Sceptics will insist that these are down to mistaken identification or hoaxes. However, on August 14th, 1966 two ex-police photographers snapped this large feline in Worplesdon, Surrey. Around the same time a farmer claimed to have shot and injured a big cat in the area but could provide no evidence to this effect. Reported sightings trailed off until, in 1970, paw prints were found in the snow that were once again identified as those of a big cat. To this day sightings of the Surrey puma are still recorded, but no substantive evidence has ever been found. Could there really be a big cat – or even a breeding population – on the loose in Surrey?

The puma, *Felis concolor,* is a mammal native to America. It tends to stalk and ambush its prey and feeds on mostly larger animals. It prefers hunting in enclosed areas where it can corner its prey, rather than wide open plains, and tends to hunt around dawn or dusk. It can grow up to 2.7m (9ft) long (including the tail) and 0.8m (2.5ft) tall. Males tend to weigh around 91kg (200lb) and females slightly less. Its colouring is plain – tawny with a reddish hint – and it tends to live for about ten years. Why sightings of these animals are being reported in the UK is a mystery. One theory is that people have purchased the cats as pets, only to set them loose when they grew too big or dangerous. Another theory is that there are escapees from wildlife parks or zoos roaming the countryside, but official reports of large feline escapees are notoriously difficult to confirm. Fantasy or fact? You decide.

'Paw prints were found in the snow that were identified as those of a big cat'

Cats and More Cats

On January 11th, 2003, the British newspaper *The Guardian* published the following report, written by John Vidal:

> *'Some zoologists are convinced Britain has a healthy, growing population of animals associated with Africa. Despite hoaxes, there are established "beasts" of Braintree, Balmoral, Barton, Billericay, Blairgowrie, Bodmin, Bucks., Carmarthen, Dean, Gobowen, Gloucestershire, Exmoor, Fife, Ongar, Paisley, and a dozen other places. Every county has reported sightings – from lynxes and leopards, to pumas, ocelots and jungle cats.'*

Neil Arnold, the director of the Kent Big Cat Society, claims to have received reports of over 1,500 sightings over a period of 10 years, and he and zoologists such as Quentin Rose from London Zoo, believe that there is a significant population of big cats in Britain – and that they are on the increase. This may have been caused by the Dangerous Wild Animals Act in the late 1970s forcing people to release exotic pets which then crossbred with domestic cats to produce hybrids. If this is true then the following photos need close attention.

'Some zoologists are convinced Britain has a healthy, growing population of animals associated with Africa'

Irish police released this picture on March 13th, 2008 taken by a woman near Manorcunningham, Co. Donegal. Superintendent Vincent O'Brien was quoted (in the *Irish Independent* on March 14th) as saying, 'She saw this animal up close in her garden and she knows it wasn't a dog.' The animal was snapped prowling farmland in an area where there had recently been reported attacks on sheep.

From Scotland we have the so-called 'Helensburgh Beast'. The picture was taken by PC Chris Swallow using his mobile phone on June 30th, 2009 in Helensburgh, Argyll. He managed to take a still photo and a few minutes of video. There had recently been similar sightings reported in the general area. Experts claimed that the animal was an over-fed domesticated cat.

Dubbed 'the fen tiger' (but clearly not a tiger, rather another big cat!), this animal was photographed by Ben Coles behind his house at Snailwell, near Newmarket, England, on August 26th, 2007. He described the animal as 1.2–1.5m (4–5ft) long and 0.9m (3ft) high. Mr Coles claimed that his usual scepticism had been swept away now that he had witnessed the animal first hand.

'The fen tiger' once again – this video footage was captured by William Rooker in 1994 near the Cambridgeshire village of Cottenham, some 20 miles from where Ben Coles' photograph above was taken. The footage was two minutes long.

Jellyfish Armada

There have been many tales of enormous jellyfish invading coastal waters, including the *Cyana capillata* of 1865, which had a 2m (7ft) bell and 36.5m (120ft)-long tentacles. When a number of Portugese man-of-war jellyfish (*Physalia physalis*) were spotted washed up on some beaches in the south-west of the UK in 2009, it was considered a newsworthy event. The Marine Conservation Society (MCS) issued a warning after receiving more than sixty reports of Portuguese man-of-war jellyfish. This jellyfish, which has an airbag around 30cm (12in) in length and 12.7cm (5in) in width is so named because its airbag is said to look like the sail of a 16th century Portuguese warship. Its sting, which at best is extremely painful and at worst fatal, is what caused the greatest concern for the public's safety. The venom-filled tentacles can instantly paralyze their prey, and stings from dead tentacles and specimens can prove just as nasty as from live ones. The creature is not actually a true jellyfish, but a siphonophore, a single animal made up of a colony of organisms, which normally lives far out in the ocean. It was the third consecutive year that large numbers of the species had been recorded in the UK, its usual habitat being the warm, tropical waters of the Florida Keys, the Atlantic coast, the Gulf of Mexico, the Indian and Pacific Cceans and the Caribbean Sea. Its appearance can be attributed to a number of causes, such as unusually strong wind patterns, climate change or pollution. Whatever the reason for its arrival in the UK waters, one thing is certain – if you ever come across one – don't touch!

'The venom-filled tentacles can instantly paralyze their prey'

Cornish Jaws

'Welcome to the quaint seaside town of St Ives in the beautiful county of Cornwall, England. Here you may enjoy the special daytime light appreciated by many artists both past and present; you may relax on the sunny beaches; you may swim in the clear blue sea and be eaten by sharks!'

It might seem extreme, but according to British tabloids in the summer of 2007 just such a threat was possible. A holidaymaker had been filming dolphins from Porthmeor beach, and when he watched the footage at home later he realized he had caught on film what appeared to be a shark some 180m (590ft) from where he stood. A leading shark expert confirmed the 3.5m (12ft) creature was a predatory shark, and there was a possibility that it was a Great White, immortalised in the 1975 Steven Spielberg film *Jaws*. Despite the bad press that sharks suffer, of the thirty species known to inhabit British waters only two are thought to be a threat to humans. The Blue Shark (*Prionace glauca*) grows up to 3.8m (12.5ft) in length and has been responsible for only one known fatality, while the Mako Shark, which grows up to 3.8m (12.5ft) in length and can reach speeds of 20mph (32kmph) has been blamed for several fatalities. Both of these species are found in deep water a long way from the shoreline. In contrast, the resident giant Whale Shark (*Rhincodon typus*) which grows to over 17.5m (58ft) is completely harmless to humans. Similarly the plankton-feeding Basking Shark (*Cetorhinus maximus*), which can grow to over 9m (30ft), will give you no trouble.

'A leading shark expert confirmed the creature was a predatory shark'

So was this a Great White Shark, or a case of mistaken identity? Coastguards claim that there have never been any confirmed sightings of a Great White off Cornwall while other experts have since claimed that the fin could be that of a Porbeagle Shark. Whatever the answer, the chances of being attacked by a vicious shark as you dip your toe in the sea off Cornwall next summer are incredibly slim.

BIGFOOT, YETIS & APES

It is indisputable that man has a lot in common with primates. It is important to remember, however, that there are big differences too – not the least being that primates are generally covered with thick, wiry hair and have an ability to move in ways that man could not imagine.

Perhaps because of our desire to find missing links between us and the apes, or explain anthropomorphic sentiments, there has long been considerable interest in bipedal ape-like creatures that inhabit the more remote regions of the world, from the bleak, frozen wilds of Russia to the remote Himalayas. The problems with this study are many, since the animals themselves are difficult to locate, and the ready availability of commercial 'ape suits' lends itself to hoaxing. One only has to add the interest aroused by such films as *King Kong* to understand that the task ahead of us in this chapter will be both frustrating and fascinating.

The famous Bigfoot that was allegedly videoed at Bluff Creek, California in 1967 continues to arouse suspicion and court controversy more than forty years later. The Florida version of Bigfoot is known by the less-than-complimentary title of Skunk Ape because of its foul smell, while the Sasquatch of Texas is a similar-looking creature...we think. Are these real creatures, or a heady combination of hoax, myth and folklore? The De Loys' Ape photo from 1920 is a genuine enough image that shows a real, scientifically-recognised animal...or does it? Is it a spider monkey with its tail hidden behind it, or an as-yet unknown species?

Deep from the swamps of Honey Island in Louisiana comes a mysterious footprint which, if it has not been artificially manufactured, would suggest an unidentified creature lives quite happily in the vicinity. And that's not even to mention the Abominable Snowman, or Yeti – arguably the most famous characters in cryptozoology. There have been so many glimpses of these animals and photos taken of their tracks that it is almost easier to believe that they exist than not. However, despite the beliefs of many people as to the veracity of the evidence collected, there are still those who dispute it and the occasional hoaxes and spread of misinformation do little to help the credibility of the quest to prove that a creature unknown to science just might live in the woods. The so-called 'Minnesota Ice Man' provides one such case. Now long gone, it was either one of the most important finds ever made of early man, which would have enabled incredible progress in our knowledge of man's evolution, or it was a fake that fooled a number of people for quite a long time. Unless it mysteriously reappears, we'll be left wondering.

As you work your way through this roll-call of curious characters consider how many of the species would need to be alive in order for their continuity. Is one Yeti all there is, or must there be a breeding pair somewhere? As is nearly always the case, hard evidence is rarely preserved from the scene of these sightings, so all we can do is decide whether the photographs we are presented with provide sufficient proof to enable us to believe in their existence. Are you a sceptic or a believer? It's up to you now.

Bigfoot at Bluff Creek

A Bigfoot is typically covered in dense brown hair, stands upright to a height of about 2.1m (7ft), weighs over 180kg (400lb) and is wary of contact with humans. Since the 19th century there have been thousands of reports of giant hairy creatures that fit this description. This image is a still from a video made by Roger Patterson and his friend Bob Gimlin at Bluff Creek, California, on October 20th, 1967. The creature fits the description of a Bigfoot perfectly.

There have been many hoaxes concerning the Bigfoot that have not helped sightings to be taken seriously. Bob Heironimus, a friend of Patterson, claimed that the film was actually of him in a monkey suit. Bob Gimlin maintains that this was not the case but he keeps a low profile concerning the whole matter. With the death of Roger Patterson in 1972 (who maintained even on his death bed that it was a genuine shot of a bipedal animal unknown to science) it is unlikely that we will ever find out the truth. One final word of warning, though: the film was shot at Bluff Creek!

'It was a genuine shot of a bipedal animal unknown to science'

Patterson and Gimlin were crossing the creek on horseback when they claim to have first spotted the bigfoot. Patterson's horse was scared by the creature, and it took Patterson a good 20 seconds to extricate himself from the saddle, get out his camera and start filming. Patterson claims that he was some 7.6m (25ft) away from the creature at its closest. He also claims that he pursued it when it started to move away, which would explain the very shaky start to the footage.

The middle section of the video is much more steady, with Patterson on his knees some 24m (80ft) from the creature, at which point it turned and looked over its shoulder directly at Patterson (right). After the encounter the men claim to have rounded their horses up before tracking the beast for about 3 miles (5km) before losing it in dense undergrowth.

The Skunk Ape

Sightings in Florida of this big, hairy, foul-smelling Bigfoot have stretched back to the 1920s. A strong resurgence of sightings occurred with the publication of the so-called 'Myakka photographs', taken in late 2000 by a female resident of Myakka, Sarasota County, Florida. Her matter-of-fact report to the local Sheriff's Department had none of the hysteria often associated with a hoax — she believed that the animal stealing apples from her garden each night might have been an orangutan. However, its description did not match that of an orangutan: it was described as being about seven feet tall, with dark brown/reddish hair, and 'an awful smell that lasted well after it had left…'. Some reports suggested that the cause of the foul smell might be because it lived in the county's sewers.

The photos were developed locally and, as far as anybody knows, have not been tampered with. In 2003 the creature was also blamed for the disappearance of a number of domestic cats in Tennessee. So we are left with the usual possibilities: that the Skunk Ape was in actual fact a hoax, a case of mistaken identity, or the Florida Skunk Ape was on the loose (and possibly still is).

'It had an awful smell that lasted well after it had left'

Bigfoot or a Ghillie Suit?

On November 30th, 2009 police on the west side of San Antonio, Texas, USA, received a 911 call from multiple eyewitnesses who claimed that they had seen a hairy Bigfoot, standing over 1.8m (6ft) tall, run out of the woods and kill a deer.

The officers who interviewed the witnesses found them to be completely sober and rational, though understandably scared. A caller described what she saw:

'this big thing was 23m (75ft) away from me, smelled awful, devoured a whole deer carcass, and then screamed, screeched, and took off across the street.'

'This big thing devoured a whole deer carcass, and then took off and screamed'

Sightings of this Bigfoot appear to have started in 2005 and have enjoyed a recent resurgence in this particular part of the world. It has been suggested that this picture is a hoax, however, as the creature amongst the trees could also bear some resemblance to a ghillie suit that is designed to be used for camouflage. The suit is worn by the person wanting to be concealed in the foliage. Without further information or hard evidence, it is very difficult to decide whether this really is a Bigfoot standing in the woods or a case of high jinx.

De Loys' Ape

In 1920 François de Loys, a Swiss geologist, was searching for oil near the Tarra river on the Columbia/Venezuela border when he and his colleagues were attacked by a pair of these creatures while camping one night. He shot one, and the other fled. The photo allegedly shows an ape 1.5m (5ft) tall, covered with reddish hair, sitting on a crate and propped up by a stick. The creature reportedly had 32 teeth, and no tail. It was not possible to bring the carcass back with him, which could surely have been the only possible proof that these apes existed in the Americas.

Unofficially known as *Ameranthropoides loysi* (named by the anthropologist Georges Montandon) the existence of this photo was not revealed by De Loys until 1929. However, the Paris Academy of Science labelled it a hoax consisting of the corpse of a spider monkey (*Ateles belzebuth*) with the tail concealed behind it. Despite other claims of similar sightings (Roger de Courtville in 1938 and 1947) it is generally believed to be a hoax. Sceptics claim that by not photographing the posterior of the creature de Loys cannot prove his claim that the animal had no tail, and other clues have since come to light, such as a banana tree stump in the shot, that suggest de Loys may not have taken this photograph where he said he had. Whether this is a large spider monkey, an innocent hoax to liven up a difficult expedition, or a more sinister, political attempt at explaining evolution, the creature really is quite bizarre to look at, and I defy anyone not to be scared rigid if approached by it one night!

'The creature had 32 teeth, and no tail'

Bigfoot or Bear?

Rick Jacobs, a hunter from Pennsylvania, USA, claims to have taken this picture when he was in the Allegheny National Forest intending to record deer. He reportedly hung his camera in a tree and closed the shutter, using an automatic trigger. The photo was posted on the website of the Bigfoot Research Organization, where it was claimed to resemble a young Sasquatch – a Canadian term for Bigfoot.

The Pennsylvania Game Commission (PGC) investigated the photo, which was taken at a secret location in the forest, and declared it to be a bear with a severe skin disease. Without further verification from Mr Jacobs or evidence to prove to the contrary it is hard to believe that this is a Bigfoot that has been caught on camera, especially in light of the PGC being experienced at identifying such photos. But wouldn't it be great if all those sceptics were wrong?

'He hung his camera in a tree and closed the shutter, using an automatic trigger'

Honey Island Ape

The three-toed footprint shown here allegedly belong to the Honey Island Swamp Monster, located near New Orleans in Louisiana, USA. The first claimed sighting was in 1963 by Harlan Ford, an air traffic controller who had entered the deep woods of the swamp with a friend to try to locate a camp. Thinking they had found the site, the men stumbled through the undergrowth to the clearing to be confronted by the ape, which was staring straight at them. Their startled voices scared the creature, which fled into the dense woodland. Harlan and his friend gave chase but were only able to find the creature's tracks, which we see here.

These footprints, with three or possibly four toes, do not resemble other claimed Bigfoot prints, and this classification may not be correct. Neither, however, do they resemble the footprints of any other common animal. A local legend recalls a train crash when allegedly some chimpanzees from a circus escaped from the train that may have now interbred with other local creatures to produce hybrids. As ever, the existence of this creature is hotly contested, with local residents divided in their opinions. The only way to answer the puzzle once and for all is to find the animal that left these curious footprints.

'The men were confronted by the ape, which was staring straight at them'

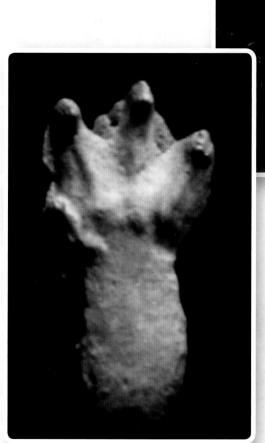

Could it be a Yeti?

The Yeti – or Abominable Snowman, as it is also known – is arguably one of the most famous characters of cryptozoology. Widely believed by scientists to be the stuff of myth and legend, the most common areas for reported Yeti sightings are around Mount Everest, Nepal and the bleak lands of China and Russia to the north of the Himalayas. There have been many claimed sightings since the 19th century and numerous expeditions have discovered tracks that have not been identified as any known animal. The information gathered suggests the existence of at least three types of bipedal animal, some of which weigh in excess of 77kg (170lb) and reach an upright height of 2m (7ft). Of the many possible reports that could be cited, this one by a professional mountaineer is typical:

'Before 1951, though like other travellers I had seen several sets of inexplicable tracks in the snows of the Himalayas and Karakoram, and had listened to innumerable stories of the 'Yeti' told by my Sherpa friends, I was inclined to dismiss the creature as fantasy. But the tracks which Michael Ward...and I found in the Menlung Basin after the Everest Reconnaissance Expedition, were so fresh and showed so clearly the outline and contours of the naked feet that I could no longer remain a sceptic. There could be no doubt whatsoever that a large creature had passed that way a very short time before, and that whatever it was it was not a human being, not a bear, not any species of monkey known to exist in Asia.'

(Eric Shipton in the foreword to *The Snowman and Company*, Odette Tchernine)

'The tracks were so fresh and showed so clearly the outline and contours of the naked feet'

This is one of Shipton's footprints, measuring 33cm (13in) in width and 46cm (18in) in length. It was found on a trail that Shipton, Ward and their guide Sen Tensing followed over the Menlung Glacier between Tibet and Nepal for about 0.5 miles (0.8km). Reactions to the find were mixed, with some accusations of misidentification and hoax among other claims that evidence for the existence of the elusive Yeti had indeed been found.

There is considerably less information available for this image that was allegedly taken by two hikers in Nepal in 1996. It is somewhat blurred, and without further details it must remain a possible but unverified sighting. Are you with the sceptics or the believers?

The Minnesota Iceman

In 1967 a showman, Frank Hansen from near Winona, Minnesota, USA, was exhibiting a 'hairy man' in the Milwaukee area that he claimed was the 'missing link' between apes and humans. The exhibit was spotted by Terry Cullen, variously described as a zoology major as well as a snake dealer who, having failed to obtain interest in it from local academics, eventually contacted Ivan Sanderson, a zoologist and expert on the Abominable Snowman. By chance, the cryptozoologist Bernard Heuvelmans was staying with him at the time and so the two of them travelled to Hansen's farm to inspect the animal that was frozen in a block of ice. Hansen was vague about the details of his acquisition of the creature and wary of any in-depth investigation of it. Sanderson and Heuvelmans inspected the exhibit for several hours over a period of three days, taking photographs and making detailed drawings. During this time they became increasingly convinced that the creature was genuine, as signs of putrefaction became evident as some of the ice melted – Heuvelmans even named it *Homo pongoides*. He described it as resembling a male, just under 1.8m (6ft) tall, excessively hairy, with a pug-like nose, short legs and flat feet. The specimen was lying on its back with the left arm twisted behind the head and the palm of the hand upward. Facial injuries suggested that it had been shot through the head.

'It was excessively hairy, with a pug-like nose, short legs and flat feet'

As scientific papers were written about the Iceman the media started taking an interest. In 1969 it emerged that the original body had mysteriously disappeared and the owner had replaced it with a model. Sanderson nicknamed the specimen 'Bozo' (a television clown) and the hoax speculations increased. In a 1995 interview Hansen reported that he 'never did find out if the iceman was genuine'. So the question remains: Was the Minnesota Iceman really an example of early man trapped in ice or just a model?

A Big Hairy Beast

Justyna Folger was entering a river in the Tatra Mountains, Poland, when a large, hairy animal revealed itself to her and was indistinctly caught on film by her boyfriend Tadeusz Serafinowski. The images shown here came after this sighting in the same district. These stills were taken from video footage made by Piotr Kowalski on August 28th, 2009 as he was videoing a goat on a mountain path. He explains:

'I saw this huge ape-like form hiding behind the rocks. When I saw it it was like being struck by a thunderbolt. Coming from Warsaw, I never really believed the local stories of a wild mountain ape-man roaming the slopes. But now I do.'

The figure allegedly ran into view and was later described in the *Fortean Times* by Robert Bernatowicz, the President of the Nautilus Foundation in Warsaw as follows:

'It shows something that moves on two legs and is bigger than a normal man – but because the camera shakes so much it is difficult to say what it is. We need to go to the site and see what traces, if any, are left.'

Sound advice indeed but with the time that has elapsed it is inevitable that, as so often happens, vital evidence will have been lost, and we are left to decide whether we believe Mr Kowalski's account or not...

'I never really believed the local stories of a wild mountain ape-man roaming the slopes'

'I never really believed the local stories of a wild mountain ape-man roaming the slopes'

LIVING DINOSAURS

We have maintained a fascination for dinosaurs and prehistoric animals for many, many years. Plastic models continue to be popular gifts for young boys, with books and fantastic museum collections continuing the fascination. Films like *Jurassic Park* and *The Lost World* have fuelled people's interest and the signs are that this enthusiasm will not be extinguished.

Dinosaurs were land creatures that lived in the Mesozoic Era from 65 to 225 million years ago. The era breaks down into three periods: the Triassic, Jurassic and Cretaceous. The well-known flying and swimming species were actually reptiles, but they are traditionally grouped together with the 'terrible lizards' we all know and love! This is not a book on palaeontology and if you wish to further your knowledge in this direction then there are many books to choose from. Be warned, however – the world of the dinosaurs is full of confusion, speculation and controversy. Fossils can only tell you a limited amount, and since humans were not around at the same period (except in fictional accounts) we are unlikely to read a first-hand account of life in the Mesozoic. But have a few dinosaurs survived and are lurking in the earth's most remote and secretive areas? Maybe.

The 'pterodactyl' shown in this chapter is almost certainly a fake, but that doesn't mean that all sightings of flying reptile-like creatures are based on hoaxes or mistaken identity. Trying to photograph a flying anomaly in a remote African jungle is next to impossible – especially if there are very few of them in existence. Most of Australia is unexplored even by native aborigines, so the 1984 discovery of the footprints of what appeared to be a large bipedal reptile, referred to as 'Burrunjor', was quite a scoop. The Stegosaurus image found on an eight hundred year old temple in Cambodia has stirred up considerable controversy. Is it simply a dragon from folklore or myth being sculptured here, or were there one or more stegosauruses wandering around Asia at the time?

This chapter is intentionally confusing as the information for some of the remaining images contradicts itself. We have the so-called Kasai rex from the African Congo shown as a probable cut-out of a photo of a monitor lizard, and then an even more improbable T. rex attacking a rhinoceros. The Emela-ntouka is claimed to resemble the frilled Styracosaurus, but its common description with one horn suggests the Monoclonius – or perhaps literally a rogue rhino. With Mokele-mbembe we have a water dwelling sauropod dinosaur-like creature that may be an elephant with its trunk raised out of the water. Sanity is returned with the image of the woolly mammoth about which a considerable amount is known through several well-preserved specimens having been found in and around Siberia. Solid evidence at last! The question remains as to whether the species has survived to the present day.

The 'Civil War' Pterodactyl

The late 19th century produced some curious claimed sightings of the infamous flying dinosaur, the Pterodactyl. This particular image is said to show a group of US Civil War soldiers from the 1860s, with one of these creatures stretched out at their feet. The *London News* of February 9th, 1856 ran a story from France of a group of miners blasting into a cave when a 'leathery creature' with a 3m (10ft) wingspan emerged and promptly died. There is no evidence to support this amazing account. Natives of sub-Saharan Africa claim that they are occasionally attacked by a creature they call the Kongamato which is said to resemble a large Pterosaur. Photos of the creature have never been taken, however. Legends of the 'Thunderbird' of North America persist to this day, with the bird reported to reach sizes of 2.5–4.5m (8–15ft) in height. Unfortunately there is no evidence to corroborate the claims.

This Civil War photo was in fact a promotional stunt to develop interest in a television programme, *Freaky Links*, which was first broadcast in 2000 on Fox TV in the USA. Perhaps the flying reptiles of the Cretaceous Period and before have truly died out, but just because this image is a hoax it doesn't necessarily mean that they all are, does it?

'A leathery creature with a 3m (10ft) wingspan emerged and promptly died'

Burrunjor

In 1984, huge three-toed footprints from a gigantic bipedal reptile were found near Narooma, New South Wales, Australia. The researcher, Rex Gilroy, confirmed the find and made a plaster cast of one of the tracks, which measured 0.6m (2ft) in length and 15cm (6in) wide. Reports of tracks being found, cattle stock on droves being mutilated and men and animals being frightened first emerged in the 1950s. Then, in 1970, some nine years after the claimed sighting, Johnny Mathews (a part-Aboriginal tracker) claimed a sighting of a 7.5m (25ft) -tall monster:

'Hardly anyone outside my own people believes my story, but I know what I saw'.

The Burrunjor has been described as a large bipedal, three-toed, animal-eating reptile with short arms. This inevitably brings to mind the image of a Tyrannosaurus Rex, one of the largest land carnivores of all time. It is worth remembering that much of Australia is remote desert and little explored, so there is a distinct possibility that one or more creatures live there that are to this day unknown to science. If Burrunjor are more than an aboriginal folklore tale then one must accept the possible survival of a Cretaceous dinosaur, even if it has evolved into a new species. Does T. Rex live on in Australia, or is the creature part of the country's rich folklore?

'There is a distinct possibility that one or more creatures live there that are to this day unknown to science'

A cast made from the three-toed footprints found near Narooma, Australia. It is thought they belong to the Burrunjor, a three-toed bipedal.

Gef the talking Mongoose

In 1931 it came to the media's attention that it was being claimed that a weasel (later described as a mongoose) was talking to the inhabitants of an isolated farm in Doarlish Cashen, Glen Maye on the Isle of Man. The Irving family, who owned the farm, consisted of the husband and wife and a thirteen-year-old daughter called Voirrey. Gef, as the mongoose became known, was held responsible for a variety of noises and sounds, including 'a shrill scream' that was heard on numerous occasions. It is also reported that the mongoose developed the ability to talk, and Jim Irving (the father) kept a diary of the activities and conversations had with Gef, which also included performances of the song Home on the Range. Voirrey, who was the only person able to catch a glimpse of Gef, claimed that he had told her that he was born in New Delhi, India, in 1852. She managed to take the rather blurred image of Gef shown here, and some hairs from his fur and alleged footprints were sent away for analysis.

The hairs turned out to be from the family dog, while paw prints and teeth marks were also discredited by the Natural History Museum in London. As Gef's activities and language became more outrageous the lack of hard evidence finally broke the boggle barrier of the investigators, and Gef was forgotten about. More than one of them felt that Voirrey was behind this phenomena and, for once, we probably should agree with them.

Gef, as the mongoose became known, was held responsible for a variety of noises and sounds, including 'a shrill scream' family with whom the creature lived, it gave direct answers to questions and made spontaneous comments – some of them quite witty and knowledgeable.

The animal haunted a place called Doarlish Cashen, an isolated farmstead perched over 700 feet (213 metres) up on the west coast of the island. It was a treeless terrain without trees or shrubs. Even the nearest neighbours were out of view, over a mile (1.6 kilometres) away. Ordinarily there would be little to attract anyone to Doarlish Cashen. But, in September 1931, the rumours of the talking weasel sent the journalists scrambling up the forbidding hill to meet the Irving family who lived at the farm.

A clear picture of Gef, the talking mongoose – centre of a media sensation in the early 1930s. Usually Gef would not show himself even to the family with whom he lived – or whom he haunted – on the Isle of Man. But, so the family said, he allowed this photograph to be taken by Voirrey Irving, the daughter of the house. This wonderful talking animal often witty and as often insulting, managed to elude all his many investigators

ing feature – two magnetic eyes that haunt the visitor with their almost uncanny power. It was all too easy to draw the conclusion that Margaret Irving was the dominant personality in the household.

The Irvings' daughter Voirrey was 13 but old for her years. She seemed a reserved and undemonstrative child, hardly a scholar but obviously intelligent. And she took an intelligent and eager interest in anything to do with animals, reading any article or book she could get that dealt with them. By contrast, she was also fascinated by mechanical devices – such as motor cars, aeroplanes and cameras.

Voirrey's knowledge of animals was not just theoretical but also practical. She was

The mongoose that talked

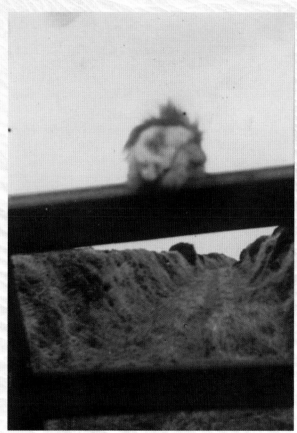

Stegosaurus

What is this image doing on the 800-year-old jungle temple of Ta Prohm, from the Khmer civilization in Cambodia? Attention was probably first drawn to it in a travel book by Claude Jacques and Michael Freeman:

> 'Among the vertical strip of roundels in the angle between the south wall of the porch and the east wall of the main body of the gopura there is even a very convincing representation of a stegosaur'.

Where did the mason find his inspiration if there was not a Stegosaur wandering around Cambodia 800 years ago? If a skeleton had been discovered then guess-work could have been used, in the same way as modern fleshed-out interpretations are made. But why is there only this one example, and why have Stegosaur skeletons not been found in Asia?

The herbivorous Stegosaurus averaged around 9m (30ft) in length and was 4m (14ft) tall, and is easily indentifiable thanks to the distinctive double row of kite-shaped plates rising vertically along its rounded back and the two pairs of long spikes extending horizontally near the end of its tail. Some of the proportions in this carving vary from what paleontologists have learned from the study of fossils – for example the head is too large and the tail doesn't have the characteristic spikes. Sceptics have suggested it could be a depiction of a rhinoceros or wild boar, with the plates representing background vegetation. Even a chameleon has been offered as an identification. Did a Stegosaurus really roam the jungles of Cambodia?

'Sceptics have suggested it could be a depiction of a rhinoceros or a wild boar'

Kasai Rex

The Kasai valley is an area of the African Congo where it is alleged that, in 1932, a Swedish plantation owner named John Johnson (sometimes spelled Johanson), was travelling with a servant when they encountered a rhinoceros. While attempting to pass it without detection (or shoot it, depending on which version you believe) they were surprised by a large creature rushing out of the undergrowth and attacking it. The predator was described as being:

'reddish in colour, with blackish-coloured stripes…it had a long snout and numerous teeth'.

He estimated that the creature was about 13m (43ft) long and was a Tyrannosaurus Rex (he probably had not heard of the more obscure, but similar, Tarbosaurus). A very similar story was published in the *Rhodesia Herald* in the same year, but both accounts contained inaccuracies that have led many people to discount them, such as the lack of native sightings, other accounts or fossil remains. But what of the photos? The 'monitor-lizard' photo (left) would appear to be a cut-out, given away by the white outline around the 'reptile'. It is equally hard to believe in the authenticity of the other photo. The scene could perhaps have been recreated with some children's toys. You decide!

'They were surprised by a large creature rushing out of the undergrowth and attacking it'

Mokele-mbembe

The Mokele-mbembe is a large, water-dwelling cryptid that inhabits the Congo River basin. Variously described as at least the size of an elephant but with a long flexible neck and tail, the amphibious nature of the Mokele-mbembe dictates that it dwells around or in water. Although herbivorous, some claims have spoken of it killing hippopotamuses and crocodiles, and even overturning canoes with its large tail. The creature, whose name means 'one who stops the flow of rivers' has a history of sightings and information stretching back to at least 1776 when Abbé Lievain Bonaventure wrote:

'it must have been monstrous: the marks of the claws were noted on the ground, and these formed a print about 1m (3ft) in circumference'.

The animal was named by Lingala-speaking pygmies from the Likouala swamp region in the Congo in 1913. The quest to find the mystery creature continues into the 21st century, but with the same frustrating results...

Could this be, as the biologist Roy Mackal maintains, 'a sauropod dinosaur'? Other possibilities are that it could be a giant monitor or even an iguana; equally, an African elephant swimming with its trunk raised might cause such a misinterpretation. Perhaps one should leave the last words with the cryptozoologist Karl Shuker:

Descriptions of the Mokele-mbembe vary but some suggest it's similar in appearance to a small sauropod dinosaur.

'If dinosaurs could exist unknown to science anywhere in the world, the Likouala is where they would be'.

Emela-ntouka

The Emela-ntouka, 'elephant killer' or 'water-elephant' allegedly lives around the swamps of Central Africa and has a similar appearance to a very large one-horned rhinoceros, but with a long, heavy tail. Its title is confusing since it is said to be herbivorous by the natives of the area, but is fierce when its territory is invaded. There have been various claims of sightings and killings, but neither a living nor dead specimen has ever been discovered.

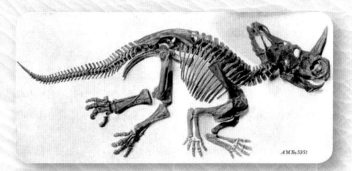

Cryptozoologists like the idea that it might be a supposedly extinct dinosaur of the beaked Ceratopsian or horned type. The main contender would be the Monoclonius with a single horn, rather than the elaborately frilled Styracosaurus or the much-loved three-horned Triceratops, which have not been described so closely. The dinosaur theory is weakened, however, since fossils of these particular species have not been found in the region, and it is generally thought of as a mammal rather than an egg-laying dinosaur. Loren Coleman, an expert in such matters, has suggested a new species of rhinoceros might have been found, but some people dispute this, mainly because of the differences in the tail. The remote and inhospitable region where it is reported to live keeps alive the prospect that perhaps a new species of animal is waiting to be discovered by an intrepid explorer. Just remember to bring back evidence, should you be the one to find it.

The Emela-ntouka is claimed to be the size of an African bush elephant and a similar shape and appearance to a rhinoceros including one long horn on its snout, and perhaps related to the centrosaurus, of which here is a nearly complete skeleton.

The Mammoth

In 1901 the Berezovka River, just inside the Arctic Circle, revealed a frozen mammoth that had been preserved so well that undigested food was found in its stomach, and in 1977 a complete baby mammoth was found in the Yakutsk region of Russia. The best preserved animals have been found in the frozen wastes of Siberia, including the one pictured, which was found in the 19th century and exhibited in St Petersburg. It would appear that the creatures flourished from 150,000–10,000 years ago, but that a dwarf variety survived into more modern times. It is widely believed that they died out as a result of climate changes and excessive hunting by increasing numbers of humans. Mammoths could reach heights of 4m (13ft), with tusks of up to 4.8m (16ft), which were used for a variety of reasons including clearing snow away and digging for food. Weights of 8,000kg (18,000lb) have been estimated.

Scientists have learned a great deal about the mammoth (*Mammuthus primigenius*) since its first study in the 18th century by Hans Sloane. Several of these curious creatures have been found in very well-preserved conditions during the last 100 years or so and, as early as 1796, Georges Cuvier believed the animal was a new species and not an elephant. Do herds of these animals still exist in isolated regions? There have been occasional claims they may roam the sparsely inhabited tundra and snow of the northern hemisphere but no scientific proof has yet surfaced.

'It is widely believed they died out as a result of climate changes and excessive hunting'

OUT OF THIS WORLD

This chapter will need the biggest helping of open-mindedness, and your 'boggle' factor will probably be well and truly stretched. It is unlikely that all of the images are genuine, but at least the photographs themselves probably are so.

Aliens are never too far away from media attention but usually they leave their flying saucers, abduct some poor soul for some fairly degrading or unpleasant treatment and then clear off back from whence they came. It was therefore particularly pleasing to discover one might have been caught on film in Chile in 2004; in Argentina in 2008; and on Ilkley Moor in England in 1987. The photos show that aliens, just like us, come in all shapes and sizes and that they are not all necessarily little green men (or women, of course). As you will see the Chilean example could be an elf, the Argentinian a gnome and the English picture (taken by a policeman, by the way) returns us to the world of little green men. These images do not provide one with proof of alien activity on earth, but they are intriguing and thought provoking as to what they do actually show us and tell us about our own thought processes. Similarly the alien 'blob' of worms could make you interested from a scientific point of view, or it might just induce horror at the sight of the slimy mass of organisms living in our sewers. When will they rise up through our plumbing in a horror film scenario?

The decimated island of Haiti was the location for a grisly find in 1740 of some relics of the 'Devil Men' of the lost Ju-Ju tribe. Despite some contradictory evidence I personally believe, or rather hope, that these are gruesome man-made models. The same is probably true of the images said to represent mermaids. No, not the alluring semi-naked maiden shown in art forms throughout the world, but man-made items fusing together dried fish, hair and monkey heads. While we are on the subject of mermaids, a so-called 'fee-jee' mermaid was said to have been displayed in New York in the 1940s. It was almost undoubtedly a fake and the current example shown is a model made for the International Museum of Cryptozoology in Portland, Maine, USA. I wonder how many people forget to mention that this is just a model and how many practical jokes in the past have become accepted as true sightings with the passage of time?

The final images introduce the infamous Chupacabra or 'goat-sucker' of Puerto-Rico and elsewhere. The power of the Internet to dispense knowledge, both true and false, is apparent here once more as the images are almost certainly of a model or computer generated creature, merged with an animal that died of mange. We might be wrong, of course...

The Montauk Monster Mystery

The information available about this marvellous discovery is contradictory and frustrating. Nothing new there! The renowned cryptozoologist Loren Coleman discovered this image on the Manhattan website Gawker on July 29th, 2008, allegedly portraying 'some sort of rodent-like creature with a dinosaur beak' found on the Montauk beach at Long Island, New York, USA. Two of the photographers who came forward were local resident Jenna Hewitt and Christina Pampalone, who claimed to have taken several photos from different angles. Their photos showed an animal about 1m (3ft) -long with the 'dinosaur beak' showing what may have been signs of muzzle deterioration. Claims of a hoax, an alien, animal experimentation and natural decomposition of a racoon could easily have been verified or dashed if the carcass had not suddenly and mysteriously disappeared.

Since the original discovery a new monster was washed up at Gurney's Inn at Montauk over the July 4th weekend in 2009, which was even more gruesome than the first and smelled atrocious. In September of the same year another was evidently beaten to death in Panama, although this one bore very little resemblance to the Montauk specimens. So what is it? Without a detailed autopsy by a zoologist it is impossible to say, but if it is not simply a cleverly contrived prop then some type of carnivore would be implied by the shape of its teeth. Arguments for it being a decomposed racoon, or even domestic pet, are plausible. But maybe, just maybe, we really do have an alien in our midst?

'It was even more gruesome than the first and smelled atrocious'

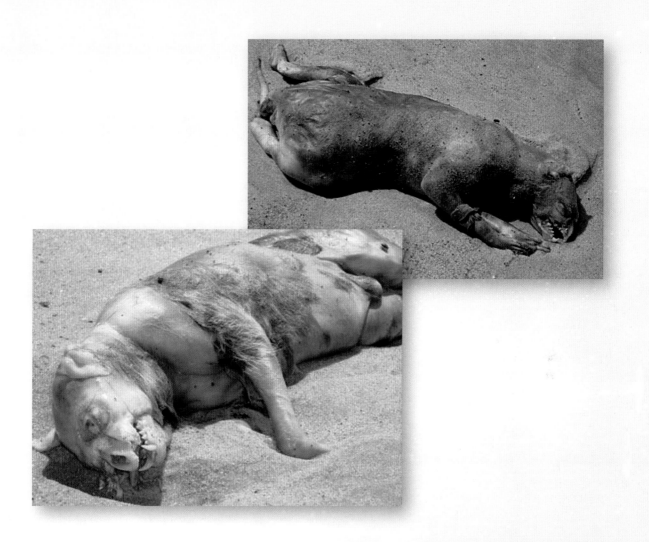

Alien?

The setting for this scene is Forest Park, Santiago, Chile on May 10th, 2004. Civil engineer Germán Pereira took approximately ten photos of the view showing two mounted carabiñeros (police) who were about 20m (66ft) away. He used a zoom lens, hence the blurring. When he was reviewing his snaps later in the day he noticed something crossing behind the carabiñeros that he neither recognized nor remembered seeing at the time. He sent a copy to the Corporaçion de Investigaçion de Fenomenos Aeros (a UFO research group from Chile) and they labelled it as an alien sighting. Mr Pereira is adamant that his photo is not a hoax, and that he has captured something unusual on film. As to its nature, he leaves that for others to decide.

If, for the sake of discussion, one discounts a hoax, then what are we left with? It certainly looks like some kind of bipedal creature and, while the perspective is difficult to clarify, it doesn't look like a child. Could it be a case of digital manipulation, or a unique photo of an alien going for a stroll in Forest Park. Over to you!

'He neither recognized nor remembered seeing an alien at the time'

Clahuchu and Bride

In 1917 Dr Henry Garfit and his excavation crew of Haitian natives were digging the oldest sections of a burial ground in Haiti when the contractors suddenly fled from the scene. Dr Garfit went to investigate the cause of their terror, and was the first to see the find dubbed 'Devil Baby'. The operation was immediately shut down, and Dr Garfit reported his find to the military authorities. When they reached the site to recover the find, however, it had completely vanished. Dr Garfit then caught a plane home but his plane plunged into the ocean en route to the USA. In 1952 the creatures were rediscovered in a voodoo temple in a Catholic church on the island. The find was saved from the pyre by one Father Alaux, who also died mysteriously in 1991. The creatures are widely claimed to be the last of the lost Juju tribe of Devil Men – a Nigerian tribe of the Yoruba culture said to have 600 gods who are also demons. The exhibitor claims that X-rays revealed that the skin, horns and hooves were human. Many legends, deaths and disappearances are attached to these artefacts and are bound up with voodoo practices.

Opinion is divided about whether Clahuchu and his bride are simply freaks of nature or the remnants of a lost race. Their present whereabouts are not known – their last known owner died in a car accident when his brakes failed.

'The creatures are widely claimed to be the last of the Ju-Ju tribe of Devil Men'

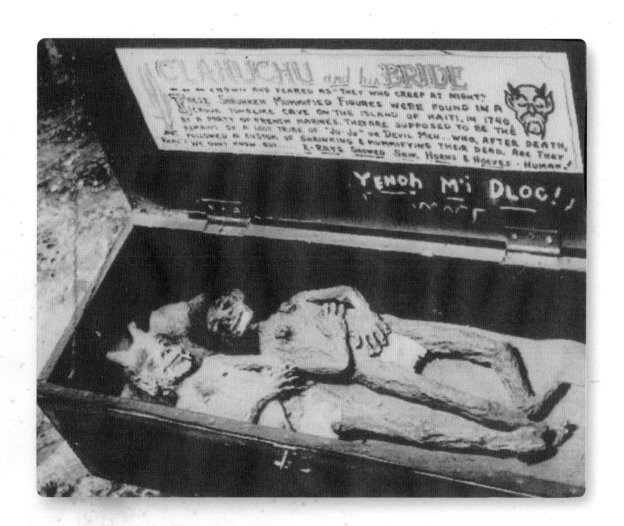

Yorkshire Alien

Early in the morning of December 1st, 1987 a man was taking landscape pictures on the moor above White Wells, near the West Yorkshire town of Ilkley, England. He claimed that:

'Something caught my eye…about 6m (20ft) away I saw what I can only describe as a small green creature moving quickly away…[I] shouted "Hey." When it was about 12–15m (40–50ft) away it turned and seemed to be waving me off. I quickly brought the camera up and took a photograph…[he then saw] 'a large object like two silver saucers stuck together…[that] shot straight up into the clouds'.

For some inexplicable reason he didn't manage to photograph the 'saucers' but recorded this single image. He also revealed, under hypnosis, that he had no memory of a period of time that day, suggesting to some that he may have been abducted.

Upon examination of the negative researchers found that it showed signs of underdevelopment, and photographic experts believed that a figure might have been later super-imposed on a background shot of the moor. The photographer's wife later declared (after their divorce) that he had made the creature out of chicken wire to fool the investigators. He denied this. Whether the alien of Ilkley Moor is fact or fiction is for you to decide – perhaps the creature will put in another appearance to back up the photographer's claims of extraterrestrial life in rural England.

'I saw what I can only describe as a small green creature moving quickly away'

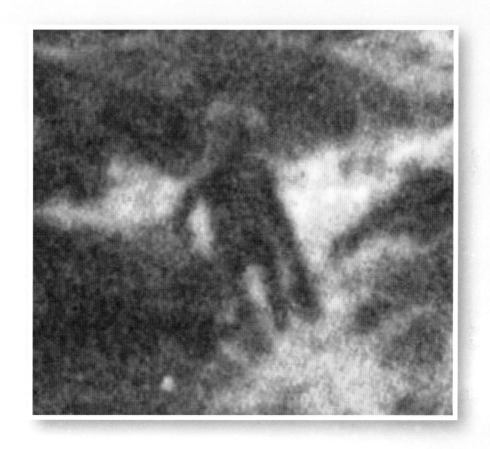

Mistaken Identities

Anja and Chris Prigg had spent the morning shopping at the markets in Hope Island, on Australia's Gold Coast. On holiday from their native New Zealand, the couple were shocked when they spotted what looked like a crocodile floating in an inland canal. Their attention had been drawn to the water by the sight of a flock of ducks being disturbed, and it was then that they managed to snap the predator.

The couple submitted their photograph to the *Gold Coast Bulletin*, but the authorities were quick to dismiss the couple's claims as lunacy, declaring that they were '99 per cent positive' that the image did not show a crocodile. To demonstrate the point, the photographs were sent to the local press and were published alongside images of a confirmed crocodile. Veteran Queensland crocodile wrangler Bob Irwin said that the Priggs' crocodile 'was probably just a log.' The last confimed sighting of a crocodile on the Gold Coast was in 1903, when a 3m (10ft) specimen was shot in the Logan River. Mr Irwin went on to say:

'There is absolutely no vegetation and nowhere for them to hide. Crocodiles are very secretive, they need vegetation and somewhere to bask. They are also nocturnal and come out at night to feed, so for them to be feeding on ducks in the middle of the day is unlikely.'

'Their attention had been drawn to the water by the sight of a flock of ducks being disturbed'

So, scary croc making an unexpected appearance or floating log? Over to you.

Croc or not? Two of these pictures were taken by Anja and Chris Prigg. The third (bottom right) was supplied by the local authorities to prove that what the Priggs had seen wasn't a crocodile, as this is what one truly looks like. Are you convinced?

Worms of Death

Olgoi-khorkhoi, the Mongolian Death Worm is a cryptid purported to exist in the Gobi Desert. It is said to resemble a cow's intestine, be bright red in colour and is sometimes described as having darker spots and blotches, with spiked projections at both ends. The thick-bodied worm is purported to be 0.5–1.5m (2–5ft) in length and is able to kill a human at a distance, either by spraying an acid-like substance or by producing an electric discharge. Mongolians say that the worm, which lives underground and only comes out of hibernation in June and July, is attracted by the colour yellow. No proof has ever been found of its existence, and some scientists believe it to be a relative of the Bobbit worm.

Though natives have long told tales of the olgoi-khorkhoi, the creature first came to Western attention as a result of Professor Roy Chapman Andrews' 1926 book *On the Trail of Ancient Man*. The American palaeontologist was not convinced by the tales of the monster that he heard at a gathering of Mongolian officials:

> *'None of those present ever had seen the creature, but they all firmly believed in its existence and described it minutely.'*

One theory is that the Mongolian Death Worm is a type of land-based electric eel, an adapted hanger-on from thousands of years ago when the Gobi Desert was an inland sea. However, no known electric eels can emit poison. Could it be a spitting snake? A legless lizard? Or simply the stuff of myth and legend?

'It is said to resemble a cow's intestine, be bright red in colour and has darker spots with spiked projections'

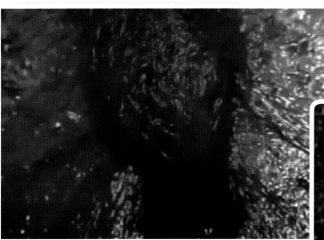

There is no evidence – physical, photographic nor circumstantial – to prove that the Mongolian Worm of Death exists. Scientists generally believe that, should it ever be discovered, it will prove to be a close relation of the Bobbit worm, pictured below.

This image above is a still from a video taken in June 2009 from a North Carolina sewer by a construction crew. It is reported to be 'a colony of worms that live in sac-like blobs attached to tree roots that grow in and around the older pipes. The sacs of worms are extremely light sensitive and all move together in response to the brightness and heat from the camera lights making them to appear to be a giant single organism.' Here's hoping they stay underground out of sight.

An Argentine Alien

One night in early March 2008, a group of teenagers was hanging out on a street corner next to the local graveyard in the San Isidro neighbourhood of General Guemes, a town in the province of Salta, northern Argentina. José Alvarez, one of the group recalls:

'We were chatting about our last fishing trip. It was one in the morning. I began filming with my mobile phone while the others clowned around. Suddenly we heard something – a weird noise as if someone was throwing stones. We looked to one side and saw that the bushes were moving. To begin with, we thought it was a dog, but when we saw this gnome-like figure emerge we were very frightened. I recorded it for a little while, and then we all took off running. This is no joke. We are still afraid to walk past the place, just like the neighbours. One of my friends was so frightened we had to take him to hospital.'

So reported the *Fortean Times*, and there have been numerous reports of similar creatures in Argentina but the questions that this report leaves unanswered are myriad. Suspicion is inevitably raised by the unidentified 'clowning around' that some of the group indulged in while the camera was rolling. Similarly, mystery surrounds the identity of the member of the group who was reportedly taken to hospital – neither do we know which hospital he was taken to nor what was wrong with him. Who are these neighbours living in fear? Perhaps the biggest question of all, however, is why, if these witnesses were as scared as they claim, did they not run away from the terrifying creature immediately?

'We looked to one side and saw that the bushes were moving'

Anthropomorphic Tuber!

This curious-looking vegetable was bought in the Shandong province of China from a market stall. It is the tuber of a fleeceflower plant, which is widely used in Chinese medicine to treat a number of conditions, from chronic malaria to premature greying of the hair. Sceptics will naturally claim that the shape has been carved or manipulated by a sharp knife in someone's hands, and perhaps it has. However, roots resembling human shapes have a strong folkloric history, most notably in the case of the poisonous mandrake (*Mandragora officinarum*), which is a member of the nightshade family and is indigenous to southern and central Europe, as well as the Mediterranean. The forked roots of the plant have often been known to resemble a human figure. It was said that it shrieked when pulled out of the ground and it was therefore recommended to be pulled out by a dog to avoid a curse. Its narcotic and other medical/magical qualities associated it with witchcraft and, in 1630, three women were executed in Hamburg for possession of it.

Whether this example is a natural phenomenon or the work of a sculptor keen to highlight the aphrodisiac qualities of the mandrake plant we may never know, but it certainly provokes debate!

'Roots resembling human shapes have a strong folkloric history'

Merfolk or Fakefolk

There have been many alleged sightings of mermaids, and folklore abounds with dubious tales about them. Sailors were lured into the depths by their beauty in much the same way that the mythological Sirens' voices doomed their listeners. Babylonian mythology included half-human, half-fish deities, and there are images of the Hindu god Vishnu taking a similar form. There have also been genuine cases of mistaken identity where seals or similar sea mammals, such as the manatee, may have been thought to be merfolk by naïve witnesses. In 1961 the Isle of Man Tourist Board even offered a prize to anyone catching a mermaid in the Irish Sea – without success. One spectacular case of hoaxing was perpetrated by R. S. Hawker, the vicar of Morwenstow Church, Cornwall, England, in 1834. He dressed up as a mermaid and swam off the coast singing as he went along.

Once again, however, the greed of humankind has led to exploitation for financial reward and many fakes have been concocted, even as far back as the seventeenth century. The circus proprietor P. T. Barnum certainly promoted such images in the 1870s and in the same century the Japanese made many fakes using monkey heads skilfully attached to fish. The October 2009 edition of *Fortean Times* is devoted to the subject of mermaids and even contains an article (by Alan Friswell) on how to make one yourself with quite startling results! As for the images here, these are undoubtedly fakes, thought to originate from the Philippines. Why someone would want to create these and leave them on a beach in the wake of a massive natural distaster is anyone's guess.

'Sailors were lured into the depths by their beauty'

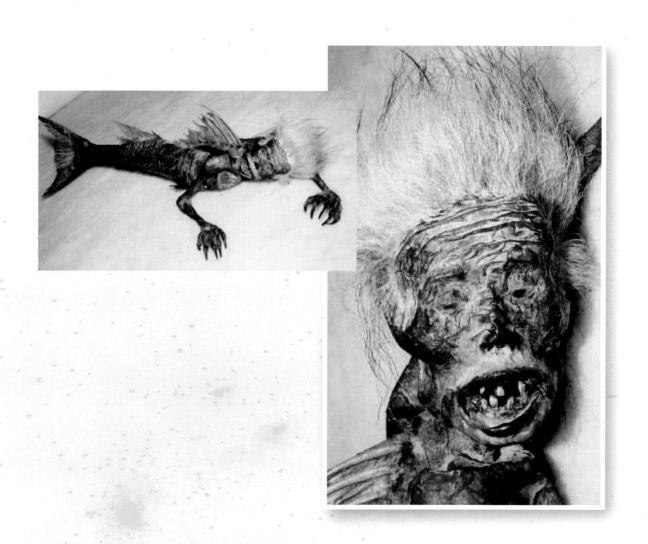

The Feejee Mermaid

In 1842, Levi Lyman alias 'Dr. J. Griffin', a member of the fake 'British Lyceum of Natural History', brought to New York City an allegedly real mermaid, which he claimed was caught near the Fiji (sometimes spelled 'Feejee') Islands in the South Pacific. The creature was 'authenticated' by the press and P. T. Barnum – a famous American showman and shrewd businessman who made vast sums of money from promoting hoaxes – showed great interest, which is not surprising since Lyman was secretly working for him. It was finally displayed on Broadway amidst considerable interest and disagreement concerning its authenticity. The public who came to see the 'mermaid' were expecting a beautiful young woman, but instead were greeted by 'the very incarnation of ugliness…[with] the withered body of a monkey and the dried tail of a fish.'

It later transpired that the model had been borrowed from a Boston showman, Moses Kimball, who had possibly acquired it from a Japanese fisherman in 1810. Although the original has long gone – probably destroyed by a fire at Barnum's museum in 1860 – the idea of the mermaid is still very much alive. The current example was created by Erik Gosselin, a special effects artist and sculptor from Quebec. It is housed in the International Museum of Cryptozoology, Portland, Maine, USA.

'The public who came to see the mermaid were expecting a beautiful young woman'

Chupacabra

In March 1995 the bodies of eight sheep were discovered in Puerto Rico, with the blood completely sucked out of them. Reports of similar killings then followed, with estimates that some 150 livestock had met their death in the same way, leading to the mysterious creature being named 'Chupacabra' – the 'goat-sucker'. Widely varying descriptions have included a grey colour, possibly bipedal and around 1.2m (4ft) tall, vicious teeth and spindly limbs. There have been sightings from 1975 up to the present day, with a number of reported attacks in the 1990s. Bodies of possible culprits have been discovered which, in some cases, have suggested known mammals suffering from severe cases of mange – a parasitic skin disease in mammals that leads to balding.

The internet has been responsible for a dissemination of knowledge regarding this legendary cryptid, mixed up with hoaxes and general mass hysteria, with dozens of pages devoted to the phenomenon. Sceptical explanations of Chupacabra include feral dogs, coyotes and monkeys, with the bizarre ranging from government cover-ups of escaped aliens to occult rituals! The image shown here can be widely found on the internet and it's provenance is disputed. Whether this vampire is the stuff of legend or an unidentified creature remains to be seen – one thing we are certain of, however, is that Chupacabra memorabilia is big business in the Americas.

'The bodies of eight sheep were discovered with the blood completely sucked out of them'

These images are taken in East Texas and are somewhat indistinct through the allegedly foggy conditions. It has canine characteristics and appears to have hair, but one needs to be ever watchful of interpreting photos that may have a perfectly normal explanation as showing something far more exciting.

Chupacabra

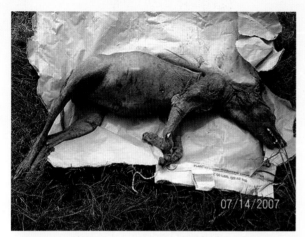

In contrast to the hairy/furry chupacabra are the images of the bald variety. This poor creature was hit by a car and killed on Buenger Road off U.S. Highway 183 south of Cuero, Texas in July 2007. One Phylis Canion explained that she had seen this animal on her property for some two years.

THE CREATURES THAT TIME FORGOT

Let us rejoice that through the efforts of a relatively few scientists and cryptozoologists, there are a number of species that have been discovered after long having been thought to be extinct. Some of these may come as quite a surprise when you learn how recently some have been discovered. For instance, the chimpanzee (1834), the giant squid (1857), the giant panda (1868), the okapi (1901), the mountain gorilla (1902) and very recently the giant muntjak (1994), along with over one hundred new frog species since 2002. Before this book reaches your shelves there may be other important revelations that will allow the 'extinct' tag to be taken away.

If just one creature had to represent all the returns from the supposed dead, then the coelacanth would top my list. Before 1937 it was believed most decidedly extinct as far as science was concerned, but increasingly since then (albeit in small numbers) it has been found swimming in our vast oceans, its appearance unchanged for many millions of years. If we stay with the secrets of the seas the frilled shark was another deep sea fish that was believed extinct but continues to be sighted in the 21st century. What other secrets do our oceans hold?

If it is difficult to study fish because of the vastness of the world's water, imagine the difficulty of investigating the habitats of the insect kingdom. One such creature, of many possible candidates, that has been included here is the Gracilidris ant – believed to be extinct for about fifteen million years until its discovery in 2006.

Land-based animals are probably the easiest to investigate despite the denseness of some forests and the lack of exploration of large areas of land on many continents. In 2000 the Brazilian Amazon region gave up another secret with the appearance of the giant peccary – a type of pig or boar. The Cuban solenodon is a very strange creature with a long, thin snout and scaly tail, recently believed extinct but then re-discovered in 2003. Alas, it would appear that mankind has hunted the 'Tasmanian Tiger' (or wolf) into extinction, but there are still reports of the Thylacine from remote regions of Tasmania and Australia.

Finally, I must mention one of my favourites – the Komodo Dragon. At the start of the 20th century the idea of dragons was firmly entrenched in the world of folklore and mythology. Hardened sceptics would not believe that a 3m (10ft), 68kg (150lb) monitor lizard stalked the islands of Indonesia until it was verified in 1910 and two living specimens were brought back to the west in 1926. Let us always keep an open mind, but continue to search for evidence before we close the doors on the existence of life under, and above Mother Earth.

The Coelacanth

Had this book been written in 1937 some members of the scientific community would have heaped a certain amount of scorn on the idea that a Devonian period lobe-finned fish belonging to the suborder crossopterygians from about 350 million years ago might still be alive and well in our seas. This all changed in 1938 when the crew of the trawler *Nerine* caught a dead coelacanth in their nets off the coast of Cape Town, South Africa in the Indian Ocean. It weighed about 57kg (126lb) and was 1.5m (5ft) long. What followed is worthy of a book in itself but, briefly, the captain of the ship contacted Marjorie Courtney-Latimer, the curator of the East London Museum who believed it to be a genuine coelacanth. It was named *Latimeria chalumnae* in her honour and its identity finally confirmed by the leading ichthyologist, Professor J. L. B. Smith of Rhodes University, Grahamstown, South Africa. However, with the catch badly decayed and the internal organs missing, doubt was thrown upon the identification, so Smith offered a reward of 100 British pounds to anyone who found another example of the species.

'The catch was badly decayed and the internal organs missing'

In 1952 a British fisherman, Eric Hunt attended one of Smith's lectures in Zanzibar, Africa, and became fascinated by the mysterious creature. He posted details of Smith's reward on posters all over the Comoros Islands, in the Indian Ocean. A local fisherman approached Hunt with a large bundle containing what locals called 'Gombessa', a grouper-like fish that often turned up in the waters off Mozambique, and which had been caught by hand-line earlier that day. Hunt salted the fish and injected it with Formalin to preserve the precious internal organs, before setting sail to Pamanzi, Mayotte to meet a delighted Smith, who had flown to meet him, and who identified the find as a coelacanth.

A coelacanth in all its beauty (left). Hundreds of examples have been found since the excitement of Smith's quest (pictured in the foreground below, with the 1952 find), and in the last ten years findings have suggested a second species thriving off the coast of Indonesia. Locals have been aware of these fish for many years, both eating them and using their skin for industrial and commercial purposes, unaware of their scientific importance.

Prehistoric Ant

Gracilidris pombero is a genus of South American dolichoderine ants, formerly believed to be extinct. Its name refers to its slender body (gracilidris) and a mythical nocturnal figure in Guarani folklore (pombero). As can be seen here, the ants have a distinct body shape with large eyes. A fossilized example was found in amber in the Dominican Republic which provided some details of the insect, but it did not allow precise examination.

However in 2006, approximately fifteen million years after it was believed to have become extinct, the *Gracilidris pombero* was amazingly rediscovered. It seems that human nature and the media prefer the discovery of larger creatures, which suggests that the *Gracilidris pombero* may not be the only small organism to be found. They may be more difficult to research due to their nocturnal nature but they are nevertheless a part of our history and importantly, our pre-history.

'In 2006, approximately fifteen million years after it was believed to have become extinct, the Gracilidris pombero was amazingly rediscovered'

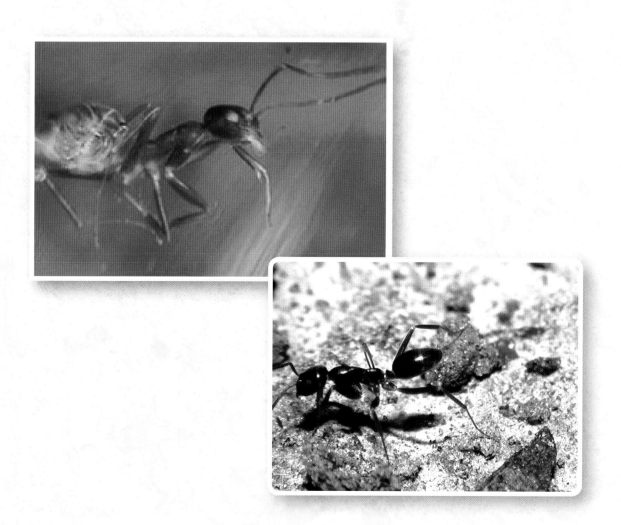

The Giant Peccary

Pecari maximus was discovered by the prolific Dutch naturalist Marc van Roosmalen in the basin of the Rio Aripuana, in the south-eastern region of the Amazon, Brazil, in 2000. It is related to pigs, boars and warthogs, but different in size and heavier. This peccary also differs from other species by often being found in pairs and maintaining a small family group. As is often the case, van Roosmalen's claim that this is a distinct species that has been in existence for one million years has met with considerable controversy.

Locals in the region where the peccary was found were aware of its existence, but not of its importance to science. There are no reports of this animal being carnivorous or attacking people but its discovery begs the question: what other strange beasts are out there, if only science was willing to fund expensive and difficult expeditions. The peccary may not be a sensational headline-making discovery, but how many other creatures are living quietly in the earth's hidden places and deepest oceans, waiting to be discovered?

'How many other creatures are living quietly in the earth's hidden places and deepest oceans?'

Solenodon

The Cuban Solenodon (*Solenodon cubanus*) is one of two species of solenodon still in existence – the other is the Haitian or Hispaniolan Solenodon (*Solenodon paradoxus*). This shrew-like creature grows up to 32cm (13in) in length from nose to tail. It resembles a brown rat but with a long scaly tail, elongated cartilaginous nose, sharp teeth and poisonous saliva. It is nocturnal and spends most of its time underground. Solenodons exist on a diet of invertebrates, earthworms and insects, as well as carrion, and are the only living mammals that can inject venomous poison into their prey through their teeth.

First discovered by the German naturalist Wilhelm Peters in 1861, it was thought to have been extinct since 1999. However, in 2003 a living specimen was discovered but, due to hunting and deforestation, it is listed as an endangered species with only 40 living examples. Little is known about the ecology of these mammals, or how they are surviving. Conservation of this species must now be of paramount importance, together with further expeditions to discover how it is surviving.

'It has a long scaly tail, elongated cartilaginous nose, sharp teeth and poisonous saliva'

The Komodo Dragon

Varanus komodoensis is the largest member of the monitor lizard family. It inhabits the islands of Indonesia, growing up to 3m (10ft) in length, and 68kg (150lb) in weight. It has no known predators except man and can live up to 50 years on just 12 meals a year, thanks to its incredibly slow metabolism. Human prey is rare but not unheard of – a tourist, Baron Rudolf von Reding Biberegg probably fell foul of one in 1974, and a child died in 2007 as a result of injuries sustained in an attack. The so-called 'dragon' received its first verification in Western science in 1910 by a Dutch administrator, Lieutenant van Steyn van Hensbroek. An expedition led by W. Douglas Burden in 1926 brought two live examples back to the West, thereby proving their existence to previous sceptics and the media. They are now a protected species and a popular attraction in zoos.

The Komodo Dragon presents us with a fine example of a creature that most people 100 years ago would not have believed existed. It does not breathe fire, nor does it fly, but it does have an uncanny resemblance to some of the dinosaurs with which we're familiar. The Papua New Guinea artrellia is a similar monitor lizard that lives in trees and drops onto the backs of its prey; it has been known to rear up on its back legs like a bipedal dinosaur and can achieve lengths of up to 9m (30ft). If proof of this creature's existence could be established rather than reported sightings of varying credibility, then perhaps these other dinosaur lookalikes will also be found to be related to the Komodo Dragon.

'Human prey is rare but not unheard of'

The Frilled Shark

The frilled shark (*Chlamydoselachus anguineus*) is a species of deep-sea shark that was thought to be extinct until it was discovered in the 19th century off the coast of Japan. Since then further examples of these very distinctive fish have been found, including one in 2007, also off the coast of Japan. This specimen was captured alive and transported to a tank for further study, but died shortly afterwards due to its inability to adjust to the warmer temperature of the water.

Although frilled sharks physically resemble eels, their gills and fins confirm their membership of the shark species. The larger females have been known to achieve lengths of over 1.8m (6ft), and are armed with many needle-sharp teeth. They inhabit deep waters around the world and are said to have changed very little since prehistoric times. They do not tend to surface regularly, but it is possible that an occasional 'sea serpent' sighting may have been caused by the appearance of such a creature. They feed on squid and other sharks and, although they are not known to attack humans, annoy them at your peril!

'Larger females have been known to achieve lengths of over 1.8m (6ft) and are armed with sharp teeth'

Thylacine

The thylacine (*Thylacinus cynocephalus*) is often wrongly referred to as the Tasmanian wolf or tiger. It is a pouched marsupial and is related to the Tasmanian Devil, measuring 0.9–1.2m (3–4ft) in length and weighing up to 36kg (80lb). The fur is brown but with distinctive black stripes on the back. Initially native to Australia, it was forced through food competition with dingoes to move to Tasmania where it fed mainly on sheep, wallabies and other livestock and small animals. Its solitary nature and increased hunting by man has led to a belief that it is now extinct. The last specimen (sometimes referred to as Benjamin) was believed to have died at Hobart Zoo, Australia, in 1936 but there have been frequent sightings in remote areas of Western Tasmania that suggest that some may have survived. In 1938 the thylacine became protected by Tasmanian law, and the UK's International Thylacine Specimen Database (ITSD) endeavours to catalogue all known surviving specimen material held around the world.

That any creature could possibly have been wiped out by man is shameful, and one can only hold out hope that these creatures may somehow have miraculously survived in remote parts of the world, like some of the other species we have seen before. If further living examples of these creatures cannot be found then perhaps the idea of cloning using data held in the ITSD should be considered...

'It fed mainly on sheep, wallabies and other livestock and small animals'

This undated photo reveals a pair of 'Tasmanian tigers' prior to their alleged extinction in the 1930s. It is said to have originated from the University of Melbourne in May, 2008

This is believed to be the embryo of a 'Tasmanian tiger' embryo from 1866. In the background can be seen the face of Professor Mike Archer. There is interest in the idea of taking DNA from it to clone the extinct marsupial which leads into the moral maze of cloning generally and its physical dangers, some would say, of playing God. One only has to think of the purely fictional results of Jurassic Park!

This photo, taken at the National Zoo in Rock Creek Park, Washington, D.C., shows a pair of male and female Thylacines received from Dr. Goding in 1902.

Picture credits

The photographs used in this book have come from many sources and acknowledgement has been made wherever possible. If images have been used without due credit or acknowledgement, through no fault of our own, apologies are offered. If notified, the publisher will be pleased to rectify any errors or omissions in future editions.

11, 13, 15, 16, 17, 21, 29, 32b, 34, 39, 46, 49t, 51, 55, 57, 64, 67, 69, 73, 75, 77, 79, 99, 101, 103, 111, 113, 117, 120, 121, 129, 133 © Unknown; 19 © discoverfishingbc.ca; 23t, 27 © 1975 Academy of Applied Science; 23b © 1933 Daily Record; 24 © 1934 Associated Press; 25t © 1951 Daily Press; 25b © loch-ness.org; 26 © Fortean Picture Library; 31, 32t © Gamma Liaison/Sandra Mansi; 33 © abcnews.com; 37t © 1964 Eric Parameter; 37bl © 1976 Edward Fletcher; 37br © Wachlin Family; 41t © cnsweb.org; 45, 47t, 47b © Fortean Times; 46 © www.bbc.co.uk; 49b © Harry Fowler; 53b © britishbigcats.org; 61, 62, 63 © Corbis Images; 71 © R Jacobs; 83 © freakylinks. com and SPR archives, Cambridge University Library; 87 © Rex Gilroy/photobucket; 93 © Eva K; 141tl, 141b © wikipedia; 95l © paranormal-encyclopedie.com; 95r © Finbar; 89 © virtualology. com; 93 © traumador.blogspot.com; 95 © Getty Images; 107l © Anjat and Chris Prigg; 107tr/ 107br © Department of Environment & Resources; 109b © NHPA; 115 © urbanlegends.about. com; 118 © photobucket; 125b © Photo by the South African Institute for Aquatic Biodiversity; 127t © www.creation.or.kr; 127b © Alex Wild; 131t © absoluterandom.com; 131b © mnn.com; 135 (all) © nationalgeographic.com; 137tr © abc.net.au.
Page 106 The details are reproduced thanks to the efforts of the respected researchers Jenny Randles and Peter Hough.

Acknowledgements

I dedicate this book to Bob Morris who I like to think would have enjoyed my foray into the world of cryptozoology. Other people have helped in various ways and, as usual, there are too many to mention all by name, but I must mention Steve and Karen for their support and my editor Neil and the staff of David & Charles. Last, but not least, you the reader is to be thanked for joining me on this voyage into the discovery of the weird and sometimes wonderful. There is so much more to learn…

Index

Loved this book?

Tell us what you think and you could win another fantastic book from David & Charles in our monthly prize draw.
www.lovethisbook.co.uk

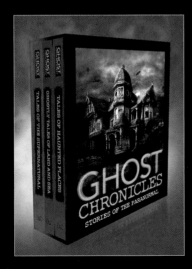

Ghost Chronicles
ISBN-13: 978-0-7153-3779-0

Three spooky volumes of classic real-life ghost stories that will make your hair stand on end.

Bibliography and references

Bord, J. and C., *Alien Animals* (BCA, London, 1981).

Bord, J., '*Bigfoot: The Hairy Man-Beast of North America*', Beyond, (February 2007).

Bord, J. and Bord, C., *The Evidence for Bigfoot and other Man-Beasts* (Aquarian Press, Northants., 1984).

Carruth, J., *Loch Ness and its Monster* (Fort Augustus, 1971).

Coleman, L. & Clark, J. *Cryptozoology A–Z: The Encyclopedia of Loch Monsters, Sasquatch, Chupacabras and Other Authentic Mysteries of Nature* (Simon & Schuster, New York, 1999).

Dinsdale, T., *The Story of the Loch Ness Monster* (Target, London, 1973).

Eberhart, George M., *Mysterious Creatures. A Guide to Cryptozoology.* (ABC Clio, California, 2002).

Ellis, R. *The Search for the Giant Squid* (Lyons Press, New York, 1998).

Farson, D. and Hall, A., *Mysterious Monsters* (BCA, London, 1980).

Harmsworth, A., *The Mysterious Monsters of Loch Ness* (Colourmaster, 1980).

Miller, C., *The World of the Unknown Monsters* (Usborne, London, 1977).

Newton, Michael, *Encyclopedia of Cryptozoology* (McFarland & Co., N. Carolina, 2005).

Parker, D. and J., *The Atlas of the Supernatural* (Prentice Hall, New York, 1990).

Randles, Jenny, *Mind Monsters* (Aquarian Press, Northants., 1990).

Stone, R., *Encyclopedia of the Unexplained* (Bookmart, Leicester, 1999).

Willin, M., *The Paranormal Caught on Film* (David & Charles, Newton Abbot, 2008)

The Paranormal Caught on Film
Dr Melvyn Willin

ISBN-13: 978-0-7153-2980-1

A mysterious and mesmerizing collection of photographs depicting ghosts and other extraordinary phenomena from around the world.

Ghosts Caught on Film 2
Jim Eaton

ISBN-13: 978-0-7153-3202-3

From shadowy figures, strange mists and apparitions to angels and demons, Ghost Caught on Film 2 is a compendium of extraordinary phenomena caught on film.

Ghosts Caught on Film
Dr Melvyn Willin

ISBN-13: 978-0-7153-2728-9

An extraordinary collection of strange and unexplained photographs that offer the exciting possibility of ghosts and paranormal activity captured on film.